HEART TO HEART RESUSCITATION

MY JOURNAL

Victor Montgomery, III, MAEd, M-RAS, CMAC

For information, contact

MSI Press, LLC

1760-F Airline Hwy #203

Hollister, CA 95023

Copyeditor: Betty Lou Leaver

Cover design & layout: Opeyemi Ikuborije

ISBN: 978-1-957354-42-2

Welcome, Warriors!

Spiritual Pathways to Freedom

People are spiritual beings. We have souls as well as flesh and bones. We all are special in the eyes of God. The Bible says we are made in the image of God. How amazing is that? Whatever a veteran's belief right now, a power greater than us all can be sought, and learning to pray is where the discovery begins. It is here where life begins again for distressed combat veterans with wounded souls. Right here the suffering, tormented soul can find relief and a reason to live. My technique of heart-to-heart resuscitation provides a safe environment that lays these important foundations and helps veterans prepare for a renewed spirit wanting to embrace life once again. Expect a miracle.

Dr. Edward Tick, the much-sought-after military psychotherapist and author would call many veterans in distress having "soul wounding and soul loss as authentic conditions". He further suggests in his writing that the efficacious counselor and facilitator should always encourage "digging deep" with their clients in order to uncover the real story details and emotions and work to transfer the moral weight of the experiences from the individual to the community.

A helpful way to address these concerns is to consider the following spiritual assumptions about trauma and pain:

Glenn R. Schiraldi, PhD., developed skills-based mind/body courses at the University of Maryland that have been found to improve self-esteem, resilience, happiness, optimism, and curiosity, while reducing symptoms of depression, anxiety, and anger. He offers fundamental evidence in his writing that suggests we may benefit from our suffering and from our triumph over our pain—and in the process become better, happier human beings, realizing that the ultimate value of pain reduction is not comfort, but growth.

Pain is a great teacher. Yet the greatest teacher imparts little wisdom if the veteran has not the eyes and ears to hear.

Warriors, if we don't work through the emotions around trauma and stress, they will gradually "eat us up" to the point where many aspects of our life will be negatively impacted forever. The moment to change is now, not tomorrow.

The only requirement to attend the H2HR Pathways Program is the desire and willingness to change your negative thinking and self-destructive behavior and to accept the fact YOU have a problem in the first place. If you are open and willing to listen to other veterans in the group, at the clinic, and to the veteran Life Coaches about the paths they took to create better lives for themselves, you are off to a good start.

- Vic

Let's begin with first things first. **Making the Commitment. Finding a Purpose.**

First Pathway

We must first admit that our war zone experiences are troubling and unmanageable to us. The combat is over, yet we continue to struggle mentally, emotionally, and spiritually. In fact, most of us share a common thread of experiences, having the same bad memories over and over: Not wanting to get close to anyone, numbing out, wanting to be alone, becoming angry and full of rage easily, and having trouble sleeping. Many of us experience muscles being tight and tense and having a sense of panic shoot through our very being. We have difficulty concentrating and often feel confused, sad, frightened, limp, and depressed. Most of the time, as veteran warriors, we mistrust others and frequently look over our shoulders—nobody there to have our back. We feel alone now. And finally, we hold on to the massive feelings of guilt about surviving the war when so many of our buddies were lost. Let us take a closer look.

Take this important opportunity to answer some very significant, up close and personal questions. These questions and your answers are for your eyes only, unless you choose to share them with others. Let's get started. (Use the extra journal pages in the back of these sections for more room to write.)

- How would you describe in words the powerlessness and unmanageability of your life? Use all the paper you need.

_____

_____

_____

_____

_____

- Have you seriously damaged your relationships with other people? If so, list the relationships and how you hurt them.

_____

_____

_____

_____

_____

- Describe any physical damage that has resulted from your current behaviors.

_____

_____

_____

_____

_____

- Describe times that you have withdrawn from social interaction and activities and isolated yourself to an extreme degree and why.

_____

_____

_____

_____

_____

- Describe embarrassing or humiliating incidents in your life. Were they related to your war experiences or memories? If so, how were they related?

_____

_____

_____

_____

_____

- Describe attempts that you have made in the past to change or control your unmanageable lifestyle. How successful have they been? Do these attempts show the powerlessness that you have over your damaging behaviors?

_____

_____

_____

_____

_____

- Do you feel any remorse from the ways that you have acted in your life? If so, explain that in detail.

_____

_____

_____

_____

_____

- Describe any irrational or crazy set of events that have happened since you came home from the war zones. Did you rationalize this behavior? If so, in what way?

_____

_____

_____

_____

_____

- Have you avoided people because they did not share in or approve of your lifestyle? If so, list these people and situations.

_____

_____

_____

_____

_____

- Can you pinpoint one time period in your life when your life began to become extremely unmanageable? If so, describe that period of time and what was happening.

_____

_____

_____

_____

_____

Goal Setting

Now that you have completed the First Pathway write down a goal that you would like to achieve. What would you like to see happen now?

_____

_____

_____

_____

_____

_____

_____

_____

_____

_____

What would you need to do to make your goal a reality? Write specific paths you would need to take.

_____

_____

_____

_____

_____

_____

_____

_____

_____

_____

Journaling

_____

_____

_____

_____

_____

_____

_____

_____

_____

_____

_____

_____

_____

_____

_____

_____

_____

_____

_____

_____

_____

_____

_____

_____

_____

_____

_____

_____

_____

_____

_____

_____

Additional Journaling

Second Pathway

Another warrior came to a group meeting and said: "I always prided myself on my hardheadedness: survival of the fittest. The fact is I wasn't superstitious or religious. I thought God as a higher power and spiritual things meant religion and that meant weird mystical thinking. I was too smart to believe in a power greater than me. What I started to realize was that if I was the greatest power in my life, I was in deep, deep trouble" – Mark, Iraqi war veteran.

We came to believe that a power greater than ourselves can restore us to sanity. And those other veterans in the local community, who are struggling with the consequences of combat-related experiences, can come together with us and influence each other in a magnificent, life changing way.

To survive this new battle, we seek meaning in having survived. We want to believe we have survived for a *purpose*. We would like to be free from distressing thoughts telling us we should never have left the battlefield alive—the place where our buddies gave their lives in war. We want to believe our lives will serve a better and higher purpose if we are alive rather than dead.

A warrior trying hard to understand his higher power said: "I have always known. My earliest memories were of looking at the world and knowing it wasn't an accident. The thoughts were too adult for a child to have, I have been told, but they are there, nonetheless. What has reinforced it is not a single event but constant protection and teaching. I can count on both hands the many times where I should by all reasoning be dead, but I survived all of them. I was led to learn many things by this inner compass. It always feels wrong to call it that, but it is as close as I can get, for now. "

Another reason for coming together here in group is that veterans who do so come to realize that they are not alone in their experiences of nightmares, flashbacks, substance abuse, anger, rage, depression, prolonged deployments, and hyper vigilance, etc. Sharing in peer-based veteran care groups with a veteran counselor leader who has actually "walked in their boots" reduces the their prior innermost need to isolate.

The second path is also a spiritual journey. This is the beginning of a new life for you. It is the basis for the problem. It is not only that the H2HR program has spiritual practicalities but also that the very foundation and success of our peer-based program is to introduce you to a renewed lifestyle that is spiritual in nature. This does not mean you have to adhere to a particular religion or practice a certain belief.

It's all about taking a step forward with real humility; your work on yourself needs to come from the heart. You need humility here. You are not God, and you cannot do what only He can do. He will cure you if you open your heart to His grace.

Following any personal trauma incident or series of events, particularly military trauma, we often face serious doubts and denial of the existence of a God or any such entity and the value of the world outside ourselves. After that last well deserved "Welcome Home," some veterans continue to "live in two worlds:" the battlefield they left behind and the one they left 12-15 months before and are trying to reenter. Juggling the combined life stressors coming from both, we doubt all our prior beliefs particularly those of any "higher power" and are often numb to our own spirituality and connectedness to the world at large and to those around us.

So pain is a way of warning. By completing these H2HR Pathways, veterans begin to realize that emotional pain was caused by them wanting people, places and things to be different than they really were or are going to be. In many instances, it is a negative, confused, and helpless reaction that is the problem. Most vets who come and begin to work the H2HR program had tried to run away from their pain, repressing it or overreacting—never any middle ground. So, they become stuck and helpless and frustrated, and finally hopelessness begins to take over their mind, body, and soul. Let us offer you a helping hand—one buddy to another. Answer the following questions, talk to your counselor, and then get started and begin to realize there is a new life waiting for you out there. Come in. We care!

Think about the following questions:

- What have been your previous experiences with religion and God as you understand Him?

_____

_____

_____

_____

_____

- Recall some of your best friends from childhood or adolescence. Describe what you liked best about them and what they liked best about you? Do you think that these qualities have any relationship to a Higher Power? Explain.

_____

_____

_____

_____

_____

- Describe events, situations, or people who have helped you to understand what a "Higher Power" or God is all about.

_____

_____

_____

_____

_____

- Describe any dreams that you have had about a "Higher Power" or God, and what they mean to you.

_____

_____

_____

_____

_____

- What have been your previous experiences with religion? How do think that this does or does not relate to your experience with God as you understand God?

_____

_____

_____

_____

_____

Goal Setting

Revisit your goal for the First Pathway. How are you progressing toward meeting your goal? Do you need to revise it?

_____

_____

_____

_____

_____

_____

Now that you have completed the Second Pathway, write down a goal that you would like to achieve. What would you like to see happen now?

_____

_____

_____

_____

_____

_____

What would you need to do to make your goal a reality? Write down the specific steps you would need to take.

_____

_____

_____

_____

_____

_____

Journaling

_____
_____
_____
_____
_____
_____
_____
_____
_____
_____
_____
_____
_____
_____
_____
_____
_____
_____
_____
_____
_____
_____
_____
_____
_____
_____
_____
_____
_____
_____
_____

Additional Journaling

_____

_____

_____

_____

_____

_____

_____

_____

_____

_____

_____

_____

_____

_____

_____

_____

_____

_____

_____

_____

_____

_____

_____

_____

_____

_____

_____

_____

_____

_____

Third Pathway

We made a conscious effort, a decision, to connect with others and reconnect with the person each of us was before the trauma. The time has come to be coached, seeking the positive power of choice versus being victimized by past experiences of war and seeking the meaning to having survived.

We must honestly and openly begin to find relief by seeking help from a power greater than ourselves, and from other people we can learn from and begin to trust. To find relief, we seek a source of help from veteran buddies whom we can learn to trust to help us renew our understandings of human emotions and spiritual qualities we fear we have lost.

And we must come to a place when we are ready to make a genuine decision to turn our will and our life over to the care of God as we understand God. We must trust in this decision.

Consider carefully the following questions:

- What is your greatest hesitation about giving up control of your life to God as you understand God?

_____

_____

_____

_____

_____

_____

_____

_____

_____

- How do you feel in general about turning your life over to God as you understand Him?

_____

_____

_____

_____

_____

_____

_____

_____

_____

- How do you think you should live your life after giving your life over to the care of God as you understand God? What changes do you expect to make and how will this look in specific detail?

_____

_____

_____

_____

_____

_____

_____

_____

_____

Goal Setting

Revisit your goal for the Second Pathway. How are you progressing toward meeting your goal?

_____

_____

_____

_____

_____

_____

_____

_____

_____

_____

Think about: How could a relationship with God, as you believe Him to be, change your life?

_____

_____

_____

_____

_____

_____

_____

_____

_____

Now that you have completed the Third Pathway, write down a goal that you would like to achieve. What would you like to see happen now?

_____

_____

_____

_____

_____

_____

_____

_____

_____

What would you need to do to make your goal a reality? Write specific paths you would need to take.

_____

_____

_____

_____

_____

_____

_____

_____

_____

Journaling

Additional Journaling

_____
_____
_____
_____
_____
_____
_____
_____
_____
_____
_____
_____
_____
_____
_____
_____
_____
_____
_____
_____
_____
_____
_____
_____
_____
_____
_____
_____

Fourth Pathway

Seeking the truth of self-inventory, a look in the mirror, we made an honest, searching positive inventory of ourselves and our actions looking at patterns of behaviors and attitudes that limit ourselves and affect those around us. A hard look in the mirror is a great place to start!

After taking the step of seeking and accepting help, we find ourselves aware of many negative behaviors and attitudes. We may fear that revealing ourselves to others will only be a negative experience. Thus, we ask a veteran buddy we trust or one of the clinic's veteran counselors, to help us see our positive behaviors and to honestly evaluate the presence of both the desirable and undesirable.

Our personal, private assessment offered by your counselor provides a free, simple, comprehensive, instrument that takes only 20 -30 minutes to complete, yet covers a wide variety of dimensions from everyday stress to life's most traumatic experiences. This completely confidential assessment is an accurate measurement of how well veterans and their loved ones are meeting the challenges of everyday living.

After taking the assessment and having your counselor discuss your profile with you, the following questions should also assist you with specific aspects of your life that may be contributing to your present anxieties, fears, and feelings of helplessness.

Commit to this statement: "To begin to heal and renew my life I must make a searching and fearless moral inventory of myself."

- Have you had any broken relationships? If so, describe them and how they hurt others or yourself. Describe any grudges, anger or resentment that you have over these relationships.

_____

_____

_____

_____

_____

_____

- What events or triggers have caused you to begin your unmanageable behaviors in the past?

_____

_____

_____

_____

_____

- Have you ever held a grudge? Did you try to get revenge? If so, explain the situation and how it played out, including whether someone else was hurt.

_____

_____

_____

_____

_____

- Describe times that you have been oversensitive. Did this ever damage your relationship with others, or were you just trying to keep your own boundaries?

_____

_____

_____

_____

_____

- Describe the faults that you most detest in others. Do you have any of these traits yourself?

_____

_____

_____

_____

_____

- Have you failed to do things that you know that you should have done? If so, then explain in detail.

_____

_____

_____

_____

_____

_____

- What are your fears? How have they caused you difficulty in your life?

_____

_____

_____

_____

_____

_____

- Describe your relationship with your friends, co-workers, or neighbors. Is there something that you wish that you could do over again? If so, explain in detail.

_____

_____

_____

_____

_____

_____

- Describe your relationships with your family of origin. Do you have conflicts with any siblings or with your parents? Are you avoiding these matters in your family?

_____

_____

_____

_____

_____

_____

- Describe the earliest memories of your life. Did you share a similar personality with those in your family or were they very different from you? Do you think that these similarities or differences caused problems in your life? If so, explain.

_____

_____

_____

_____

_____

_____

- If you were to describe your family's major themes, what would they be?

_____

_____

_____

_____

_____

_____

- Describe your relationships with your nuclear family (spouse and children) if that is different now from your family of origin. Is there anything that you wish that you could erase from this part of your life?

_____

_____

_____

_____

_____

_____

- Describe in detail any major experiences in your life that you believe changed your life forever afterwards (good or bad).

  _____

  _____

  _____

  _____

  _____

  _____

- What decisions have you made in your life that made a significant impact on your life? How did you go about making those decisions?

  _____

  _____

  _____

  _____

  _____

  _____

- Where to feel you are on the timeline of your life? Do you feel like you have wasted any precious time?

  _____

  _____

  _____

  _____

  _____

  _____

- Put your major experiences and major decisions on a timeline. Is there a pattern of any kind?

  _____

  _____

  _____

  _____

  _____

- What are you most ashamed of in your life?

_____

_____

_____

_____

_____

_____

- Do you see any patterns in your damaging behaviors and unmanageable lifestyle? If so, explain them in detail.

_____

_____

_____

_____

_____

_____

- What have you done to cover and conceal your harmful behaviors? What other deceptions did this lead to?

_____

_____

_____

_____

_____

_____

- What kind of personality do you exhibit at home? At school? At work? When no one is around?

_____

_____

_____

_____

_____

_____

- What is so shameful in your life that you would not want to tell anyone? Whom would you hurt if you told this?

_____

_____

_____

_____

_____

- Write a summary of the highlights of your Fourth Pathway.

_____

_____

_____

_____

_____

_____

- How would you like to share your Fourth Pathway summary? What details would you like to make sure that are known? Write these details down in your summary.

_____

_____

_____

_____

_____

- Describe any celebrations or honoring activities that you have done to honor the completion of your Fourth Pathway.

_____

_____

_____

_____

_____

Goal Setting

Now that you have completed the Fourth Pathway, write down a goal that you would like to achieve. How would you like to see relationships in your life change?

_____

_____

_____

_____

_____

_____

What would you need to do to make your goal a reality? Write specific steps you would need to take.

_____

_____

_____

_____

_____

_____

Revisit your goals for Pathways Two and Three. How are you progressing toward meeting these goals?

_____

_____

_____

_____

_____

_____

Journaling

Additional Journaling

Fifth Pathway

After sharing our moral personal inventory with at least one other trusted veteran buddy or counselor, gaining feedback and new perspectives is vital in successfully processing the information we are willing to share. This can be accomplished by talking with another vet or sharing our inventory in a safe, confidential and anonymous group setting, such as a community meeting.

You are not alone! Veterans with Post Traumatic Stress may have trouble with their close family relationships or friendships. The symptoms of PTS can cause problems with trust, closeness, communication, and problem solving. These problems may affect the way the veteran acts with others. In turn, the way a loved one responds to him or her directly affects the war traumatized survivor. A circular pattern can develop that may sometimes harm relationships.

In the first weeks and months, even years following deployment home from the war zones, the warrior may feel angry, detached, and tense or worried in their relationships. Veterans with PTSD or TBI may feel distant from others and feel numb. They may have less interest in social or sexual activities. Because veteran survivors feel irritable, on guard, jumpy, worried, or nervous, they may not be able to relax or be intimate. They may also feel an increased need to protect their loved ones. They may come across as tense or demanding. The veteran survivor may often have trauma memories or flashbacks. He or she might go to great lengths to avoid such memories. In fact, they may avoid any activity that could trigger a memory. If the veteran has trouble sleeping or has nightmares, both the veteran and partner may not be able to get enough rest. This may make sleeping together harder.

In this Fifth Pathway, we will admit to God, as we understand God, ourselves and to another human being whom we trust, all our angry feelings and the exact nature of our damaging behaviors. As we begin to realize more and more of our destructive behaviors and awareness that we are not alone in working through these things, all begin to become a reality that "I can do this". As we start to think more clearly, we begin to understand the reasons for our ongoing rage and other extreme emotions. We will discover that our anger and rage was likely our only defense, at the time, against the feelings of helplessness and hopelessness. These are all human feelings.

You are not odd or an outcast. You are human. And because the emotions experienced are from within, you can fix them.

Give some thought to the following questions and write down your responses:

- After working through the Fourth Pathway questions, what do you realize about your limitations and capabilities?

_____

_____

_____

_____

_____

_____

- Describe any person who has helped you to see yourself more clearly and objectively in your process of recovery and of a renewed life.

_____

_____

_____

_____

_____

_____

- What qualities would you like to see in a counselor?

_____

_____

_____

_____

_____

_____

- Describe your feelings and expectations about sharing your Fifth Pathway with your buddy, friend, or counselor.

_____

_____

_____

_____

_____

_____

- Describe what it was like in sharing the Pathway. How did you feel before, after, and during the process? Are you glad that you have done this?

_____

_____

_____

_____

_____

_____

Goal Setting

Now that you have completed the Fifth Pathway, write down a goal that you would like to achieve. How could sharing with someone make your adjustments easier?

_____

_____

_____

_____

_____

_____

What would you need to do to make your goal a reality? Write specific paths you would need to take.

_____

_____

_____

_____

_____

_____

Revisit your goal for the Fourth Pathway. How has working on this goal begun to change your relationships?

_____

_____

_____

_____

_____

_____

Think about: How could sharing with a trusted friend make life easier?

_____

_____

_____

_____

_____

_____

Journaling

_____

_____

_____

_____

_____

_____

_____

_____

_____

_____

_____

_____

_____

_____

_____

_____

_____

_____

_____

_____

_____

_____

_____

_____

_____

_____

_____

_____

Additional Journaling

Sixth Pathway

We next made ourselves ready and willing to welcome positive change and let go of old behaviors that no longer serve our confident renewed self. At this point in our journey, we become entirely ready to have God remove all of these defects of character.

We will open the doors to the past and reveal to another veteran, whom we trust, our frightening, and traumatic memories. After beginning to realize that anger is often a defense against fear, we will now begin to understand the link between the two. In this way, we can begin to accept the fact that fear is normal and relief from fear may be found by facing it with the help of other veteran buddies and your counselor.

Here are some questions to answer and share:

- Describe situations and events where you have been full of pride. What has this brought into your life that you like or enjoy? What problems has it caused you?

_____

_____

_____

_____

_____

_____

- Describe the kind of activities you really enjoy.

_____

_____

_____

_____

_____

_____

- What is some healthy eating or exercise habits that you could start?

_____

_____

_____

_____

_____

_____

- What are some unhealthy eating habits that you could give up?

_____

_____

_____

_____

_____

_____

- Describe some secret GOOD deeds that you have done or would like to do.

_____

_____

_____

_____

_____

_____

- Describe situations and events where you have been greedy, overly needy or materialistic. What has this brought into your life that you like or enjoy? What problems has it caused you? Are you ready to give these attitudes over to the care of God?

_____

_____

_____

_____

_____

_____

- Describe situations and events where you have given in to lust without regard for others or any morality. What has this brought into your life that you like or enjoy? What problems has it caused you? Are you ready to give these lustful feelings over to the power of God, as you understand God?

_____

_____

_____

_____

_____

_____

- Describe situations and events where you have been dishonest. What has this brought into your life that you like or enjoy? What problems has it caused you? Are you ready to depend upon God to keep you from dishonesty?

_____

_____

_____

_____

_____

_____

- Describe situations and events where you have given into excessive eating, drinking, shopping or covetousness. What has this brought into your life that you like or enjoy? What problems has it caused you? Are you ready to let God, as you understand God, take control of these behaviors and attitudes?

_____

_____

_____

_____

_____

_____

- Describe situations and events where you have been very envious or jealous of others. What has this brought into your life that you like or enjoy? What problems has it caused you? Are your ready to turn these situations over to God, as you understand God?

_____

_____

_____

_____

_____

_____

- Describe situations and events where you have avoided responsibility for your actions or lack of actions. What has this brought into your life that you like or enjoy? What problems has it caused you? Are you ready to allow God to help you take responsibility for your actions?

_____

_____

_____

_____

_____

- List your major defects of character.

_____

_____

_____

_____

_____

- What do you plan to do when these major defects of character begin to become evident? List each defect individually along with the proposed preventative behavior and how you will allow God to help you in your battle against these defects.

_____

_____

_____

_____

_____

_____

Important Message: *Nothing short of continuous action upon these remaining pathways, as a way of life, can bring the much-desired results.*

"Progress rather than perfection" appears as a timely reminder at moments of confusion and doubt about the realness of the Spiritual Pathways Program to Freedom.

Setting Goals

Now that you have completed the Sixth Pathway, write down a goal that you would like to achieve. How could changing on the inside make you happier?

_____

_____

_____

_____

_____

_____

What would you need to do to make your goal a reality? Write specific paths you would need to take.

_____

_____

_____

_____

_____

_____

Revisit your goal for the Fifth Pathway. Has sharing with a friend or counselor lightened your load? How so?

_____

_____

_____

_____

_____

_____

Take inventory of the goals you have set. Think about: Are you still working to achieve these goals? Which goals do you consider mastered? Make sure the goals you set target specific behaviors.

_____

_____

_____

_____

_____

_____

Journaling

Additional Journaling

Seventh Pathway

Ask for and accept forgiveness from God, as you understand God and veterans whom you trust, for committing, participating in, or knowing about acts committed which were unacceptable, causing suffering and grief for other persons and now causing you to feel tormented with guilt and self-blame. After having accepted forgiveness, we can now forgive ourselves.

We learn to ask for help and support from others. Another great dividend we may expect from confiding our character defects to another human being is humility – a word often misunderstood. To those who have made progress in the H2HR program it amounts to a clear recognition of what we have become and who we really are, followed by a sincere attempt to become what we can be. Therefore, our first practical move toward humility must consist of recognizing our deficiencies.

Repetition of new and improved behaviors develops natural responses to things which used to confuse and frustrate us. From time to time, former irresponsible responses to life's events may slip into our mind. Quickly, however, newly learned and practiced thinking and acting overpower the old ways.

Consider these straightforward questions:

- What defects will be most difficult to give up? In what order do you plan to give them up?

_____
_____
_____
_____
_____
_____

- What kind of situations, stressors, or pressures cause you to revert into your "old" defects of character? What can you do to lessen the likelihood of that stress returning?

_____
_____
_____
_____
_____
_____

- Where do you feel most supported and helped in your search for a healing process?

_____

_____

_____

_____

_____

_____

- What makes you lose hope? Can you avoid such situations? If so, then how?

_____

_____

_____

_____

_____

_____

- What (person, situation, event, thought) restores your hope? Is there a way to maximize those influences? If so, then how?

_____

_____

_____

_____

_____

_____

- What would you like to recapture in your life? Be specific.

_____

_____

_____

_____

_____

_____

- Describe in detail what you think your life will be like with your defects of character or shortcomings removed from you.

_____

_____

_____

_____

_____

_____

- What are you grateful for?

_____

_____

_____

_____

_____

_____

- When do you think life has been especially good for you? When did you have the greatest joy?

_____

_____

_____

_____

_____

_____

- Describe your typical day's activities in terms of how much time you spend on each type of activity.

_____

_____

_____

_____

_____

_____

- Have you made the correct decisions about how to spend time with loved ones, in solitude and with your flexible time? If not, how would you like to change it?

_____

_____

_____

_____

_____

- What would you do if you were granted three wishes?

_____

_____

_____

_____

_____

- What do you think you can do to make the world a better place and accomplish your mission in life?

_____

_____

_____

_____

_____

Setting Goals

Now that you have completed the Seventh Pathway write down a goal that you would like to achieve. Determine who you plan to forgive and how.

_____
_____
_____
_____
_____
_____

What would you need to do to make your goal a reality? Write specific steps you would need to take.

_____
_____
_____
_____
_____
_____

Continue to work on goals one through six, but concentrate on your goal for Pathway Seven. Forgiveness takes time. If you find yourself returning to vengeful thoughts, forgive again.

_____
_____
_____
_____
_____

Think about: *"Remember that when you forgive, you are the one who is set free."*

_____

_____

_____

_____

_____

_____

Journaling

Additional Journaling

Eighth Pathway

We seek strength and support to finally grieve for those war buddies whom we left behind. We would like to finally be free, shedding tears without being lost in unending grief. This means also being able to understand the link between grief and all the feelings we have harbored for many months and years: anger at those who left us alone, guilt about surviving while others were killed, and remorse for failing to save buddies who died.

Make a list of harm done to us or by us and find ways to restore our personal integrity. Now we must make a list of people that we have harmed and become willing to make amends to them all.

Start by answering the following questions, truthfully:

- How have you hurt yourself by acting out your emotional pain?

_____

_____

_____

_____

_____

_____

- What important relationships did you destroy or damage because of your unmanageable negative behaviors?

_____

_____

_____

_____

_____

_____

- How much time and energy have you lost from your unmanageable negative behaviors?

- What do you think you could do to redeem the time? What do you want to become?

- Make a list of all those that you have possibly harmed by your destructive behaviors. List the effect on them as individuals and on your relationship.

- Take the list of people that you have harmed and make a list of possible amends for each one of them. (To make amends, ask for forgiveness or make restitution or compensation—given or gained—for some injury or insult.)

- From the list of possible amends, choose the ones that seem most appropriate, and mark them according to level of difficulty and priority.

_____

_____

_____

_____

_____

- What consequences do you fear in making amends? What is the worst thing that can happen? What is the best thing that can happen? What is likely to happen?

_____

_____

_____

_____

_____

- Do you feel angry or resentful towards any people on your amends list? If so, write them a letter of anger, but don't send it to them. Describe here any other ways that you have used to get rid of anger and resentment towards anyone on your list.

_____

_____

_____

_____

_____

Goal Setting

Now that you have completed the Eighth Pathway, write down a goal that you would like to achieve.

_____

_____

_____

_____

_____

_____

What would you need to do to make your goal a reality? Write specific paths you would need to take.

_____

_____

_____

_____

_____

_____

Continue to work on forgiveness (Pathway Seven). Select one act of restitution at a time. Complete it, and then move forward. Since many of these also involve forgiveness, be prepared for this to take some time.

Think About: How has setting goals helped you organize your plans for a better quality of life?

Journaling

Additional Journaling

Ninth Pathway

The Ninth Pathway is the last of the "action" or "housecleaning" paths. Going to people from the past and asking for forgiveness can be frightening, but working a good H2HR program and completing the first eight pathways prepares you for the courage pathway nine requires, as you begin to make amends.

Review your list. Most of the preparation for step nine was already done when you and your buddy or counselor went through the previous step: You made your list, and you decided with your partner who you need to approach to offer to make direct amends, which are the preferred method.

We reveal to ourselves and those we trust, all remaining suicidal or self-destructive behaviors, and make a commitment to living. We wish to expose and remove those negative thoughts within us which still may prevent us from making a complete commitment to life. Thus, after further self-examination, we reveal to ourselves and those whom we trust, all remaining suicidal desires, and ask to be purged of the remaining destructive, deadly behaviors which have dominated ourselves and others. Then, we seek and accept a power greater than ourselves, God as we understand God, and daily strength to make a daily commitment to living.

It is important to make direct amends to people whenever possible, except when to do so would injure them or others.

Important questions to ask yourself:

- What amends do you think that you have already made? These can include apologies already made, helpful tasks for those that you have hurt, changed attitudes and so forth.

_____

_____

_____

_____

_____

_____

- From your list of amends, if there are apologies that you need to make, write them down here first.

_____

_____

_____

_____

_____

- • Read your apologies to another veteran or a counselor and ask them if it sounds sincere or if it sounds defensive or appears like an attack on the other person. Record here what response they have about them.

_____

_____

_____

_____

_____

- Role play with your vet buddy or counselor or other veteran friends for anything that you are going to say when making amends. Record here how these practice sessions went and what you learned.

_____

_____

_____

_____

_____

- After you have had your first encounter with making amends, record what happened here. How did you feel about it? How did the other person respond? What have you learned from this? What would you do differently next time?

_____

_____

_____

_____

_____

_____

- After you have done your first several encounters for making amends record your overall impressions here. Is there anything in common? Has anything surprised you? Has anything disappointed you? How do you feel about the process, and how has it affected you?

_____

_____

_____

_____

_____

_____

- What amends do you have the most difficulty making? What do you need to do to be able to make these amends? Yourself?

_____

_____

_____

_____

_____

Goal Setting

Write down any other amends that you found that you needed to make after starting the process of making amends.

_____

_____

_____

_____

_____

_____

_____

_____

_____

_____

_____

Write the specific paths you would need to take.

_____

_____

_____

_____

_____

_____

_____

_____

_____

_____

_____

Journaling

Additional Journaling

Tenth Pathway

Continue to reflect upon your thoughts, feelings, and behaviors in the present and become entirely committed to the healing process.

We reveal to ourselves, our higher power and another person or buddy or counselor all remaining thoughts of revenge and ask for God's strength to give these up. We seek and accept strength to give up our desires for revenge toward those who hurt us and injured or killed our buddies so we can learn the full meaning of loving one another, and ourselves.

What is a Tenth Pathway Buddy System?

The H2HR program encourages people who have completed their Fourth Pathway to do a daily inventory. As we adopt this discipline, we have found it useful to partner up with a veteran buddy or counselor to share what we have uncovered on a regular basis. Why do this?

Part of the Tenth Pathway itself involves honest communication. We recommend that you ask yourself each night: "Have I kept something to myself which should be discussed with my buddy or counselor at once?" Moreover, we suggest that when we find selfishness, dishonesty, resentment, and fear, we discuss them with someone immediately. The Tenth Pathway buddy system facilitates this kind of sharing.

In addition, the buddy system, veteran to veteran, promotes accountability. We discuss with a veteran partner the corrective measures and amends that are also a part of the daily inventory. Many of us have found this enhances our follow-through. Further, the partnership provides an opportunity for feedback and discussion that can help us through blind spots. This also happens through working with a H2HR counselor.

The Tenth Pathway veteran to veteran partnership is a valuable supplement; it allows a "peer relation" in recovery, two individuals equally supporting one another. It can also be a great way to get to know others in the H2HRprogram, outside established friendships, to extend your circle of giving and receiving help. For such reasons, we encourage working with different vet partners over time.

Here are suggestions to help develop the effectiveness of your buddy to buddy and veteran counselor partnerships:

- Make a commitment to talk to each other at least twice a week (or more at first). Less regular communication undermines the depth of the partnership, as well as the notion of discussing problems "with someone immediately." Reschedule cancelled conversations whenever possible.

- Speak with your counselor occasionally, especially if your buddy is having particular trouble with an issue. This provides information that can assist you and your counselor to be significantly helpful.

- Know where the partner is in the Twelve Pathways. Encourage moving forward. Often problems may be related to inactivity in working through the paths.

- Promote both your counselor's relationship and the H2HR program as places to expose issues and receive feedback. Alert counselors of significant problems your buddy may not be sharing.

If you are looking for a good Tenth Pathway's list to help you process a situation that you have recently been through, the following is a good exercise.

Ask yourself...

1. How was I selfish? (How was I thinking only of myself?)

2. How was I resentful? (What was the basis of this resentment?)

3. How was I afraid? (How does this demonstrate a lack of faith?)

4. How was I dishonest? (by act or omission?)

5. How did I demand to take control of a situation? ("Do it my way!")

6. How did I demand to be right? ("I told you so!")

7. How did I demand to be a victim? ("Poor me!")

8. How was I defiant? ("Don't confuse me with the facts; I've made up my mind!")

9. How was I in denial? ("I don't care; I want it my way.")

10. Whom did I hurt, and how did I hurt them? (Who was affected as a result of my action or inaction?)

11. How can I repair the damage? (How can I right the wrong?)

12. What could I have done better? (What actions could I have taken to improve the situation?)

Make a commitment. "I will continue to take a personal inventory and when I am wrong, I will promptly admit it."

Setting Goals

Think about: How setting and maintaining goals can help.

_____

_____

_____

_____

_____

_____

Set your personal goals:

_____

_____

_____

_____

_____

_____

Set new goals as needed; look back at previously set goals. Be consistent in mastering your objectives.

Journaling

Additional Journaling

Eleventh Pathway

Having strengthened our connection to others, we build relationships and meaning into all our activities.

We seek knowledge and direction from our higher power, God as we understand God, for a renewed purpose for our lives. Having been freed from those burdens which have kept us from having meaningful and purposeful lives, we are ready to find a renewed purpose for our lives. Recognizing that a higher power can also be a source of strength to live by, we will daily seek freedom from our old burdens or new problems through prayer, and meditation. In this way, we can continue to find daily freedom from the past shackles of rage, guilty memories, and impacted grief, and gain knowledge of a greater purpose for our lives and the endurance to carry it out.

In essence, we suggest that prayer and meditation put us in contact with God, as we understand God. Hopefully, that's what we've been doing with the prayers we've learned while going through the previous Ten Pathways—making conscious contact with the God of our understanding.

Now, take a moment to think about the 24 hours ahead of you and consider your plans for this time. If, when thinking about your 24 hours, you face indecision, or if you're not able to determine which action to take, ask God for inspiration and a natural thought or a decision. Remember to relax and take it easy. Don't struggle.

Through prayer and meditation, seek to improve your conscious contact with God as you understand God, praying only for knowledge of God's will for your life and the power to carry that out.

Consider these questions:

- Can you recall anytime that your life was heading in the wrong direction? If so, what brought you back? Describe this in detail.

_____

_____

_____

_____

_____

_____

- How would you describe your beliefs about God or a Higher Power to a child?

_____

_____

_____

_____

_____

_____

- What are your favorite sources of wisdom and knowledge about healthy values?

_____

_____

_____

_____

_____

_____

- Has anything you ever read convinced you to change in some fundamental or deep way? What did you read?

_____

_____

_____

_____

_____

_____

- If you were stranded on a desert island with only one book, which book would you take? Why?

_____

_____

_____

_____

_____

_____

- If you had only one week to live and unlimited resources, who would you gather around you and how would you pass the time?

_____

_____

_____

_____

_____

_____

- Write out a complete form of what you would like your legacy to be.

_____

_____

_____

_____

_____

_____

- What do you believe will happen to you after you die?

_____

_____

_____

_____

_____

_____

Setting Goals

Have you met your goal of a renewed purpose in your life.? A higher power, God as you understand Him?

Explain:

_____

_____

_____

_____

_____

_____

_____

_____

_____

_____

_____

_____

_____

_____

_____

_____

_____

_____

_____

_____

_____

_____

_____

_____

Journaling

Additional Journaling

Twelfth Pathway

If you've had the Spiritual Awakening as the result of taking the actions in Pathways One through Eleven, then you're ready to carry our lifesaving and life-changing messages to other veterans.

Having gained peace and a balanced perspective, we share our experience, strength, and hope with other veteran survivors and war buddies. Practical experience shows that nothing will so much ensure immunity from damaging behavior as intensive work with other traumatized veterans. It works when other activities fail. This is our Twelfth Pathway suggestion: *Carry this message to other warriors in distress! You can help when no one else can. You can secure their confidence when others fail.*

Life will begin to take on a whole new meaning. To watch veterans, recover from war zone trauma, to see them help others, to watch loneliness vanish, to see a veteran care group grow up in your neighborhood, to have a host of buddies and counselors in your life—this is an experience you must not miss. We know you will not want to miss it. Frequent contact with newcomers and with each other is the bright spot of our lives.

Having experienced spiritual renewal, we continue to seek our higher powers strength to love others and to help those who suffer as we have. Having had a spiritual awakening because of these H2HR Pathways, we seek to carry this message and to help all those who suffered as we have suffered.

Setting Goals

What is the primary goal to your H2HR Pathways to Freedom?

_____

_____

_____

_____

_____

_____

_____

The Pathways are a set of guiding principles in your journaling experience that outline a course of action for tackling embedded challenges related to the aftermath of war trauma relationships.

The GOAL: To learn to live a life filled with purpose and smiles and inner joy; forgiveness and a peaceful, balanced existence.

Have you reached your goals?
100%___80%___60%___40%___20%___0%___

Explain:

_____

_____

_____

_____

_____

_____

_____

Journaling

Additional Journaling

References and Resources

Alcoholics Anonymous. (2001). *The Official "Big Book" from Alcoholic Anonymous: Fourth Edition*. New York City: Alcohol Anonymous Services, Inc

Johnson, Spencer. (1992). *The Precious Present*. New York: Doubleday.

Mandino, Og. (1985). *The Greatest Salesman in the World*. Hollywood, Fredrick Fell Publishers, Inc.

Rogers, C. (1961). *On Becoming a Person. Boston*: Houghton-Mifflin.

Schirldi, Glenn R. (2000). *Posttraumatic Disorder Sourcebook: A Guide to Healing. Recovery, and Growth*. Lincolnwood, IL.: Lowell House

Tick, Edward. (2005). *War and the Soul: Healing Our Nation's Veterans from Post-Traumatic Stress Disorder*. Wheaton, IL: Quest Books

Waitley, D. (1988). *Seeds of Greatness*. New York: Pocket Books.

Warren, R. (2002). *The Purpose-drive Life: What on Earth Am I Here For?* Grand Rapids, MI: Zondervan

Suggested Reading

The Old Man and The Sea. Ernest Hemingway

Red Badge of Courage: A Novel about the Civil War. Stephen Crane

Amazing Love: True Stories of the Power of Forgiveness. Corrie Ten Boom.